马云和阿里

Jack Ma
Alibaba Dream

刘小琳　编著　　薛彧威　翻译

Sinolingua
华语教学出版社

First Edition   2018

ISBN 978-7-5138-1613-7
Published by Sinolingua Co., Ltd
24 Baiwanzhuang Road, Beijing 100037, China
Tel: (86) 10-68320585   68997826
Fax: (86) 10-68997826   68326333
http://www.sinolingua.com.cn
E-mail: hyjx@sinolingua.com.cn
Facebook: www.facebook.com/sinolingua
Printed by Beijing Xicheng Printing Co., Ltd

Printed in the People's Republic of China

前　言

　　中国是一个拥有灿烂文化的国度，无论是古代还是现代，都有许多智慧的人和智慧的事。"中国智慧故事汉语分级读物"就收集了这样一批闪烁着智慧光芒的有趣故事，题材涉及名人智慧、探案斗智、军事或商战谋略，以及科技创新等。我们根据非母语汉语学习者的阅读需求，用浅显明白、难度分级的汉语把它们一一呈现出来。让读者在学习汉语的同时，享受脑力激荡的乐趣。

　　"中国智慧故事汉语分级读物"以中学阶段及以上的汉语学习者为主要读者对象。这套读物根据语言难度划分为三个级别，每级包含若干分册，每册讲述一个中国古代或现代的智慧故事。其中 1 级为 300 词，故事长约 2500字；2 级为 400 词，故事长约 3500 字；3 级为 550 词，故事长约 4500 字。构成故事的词汇均来源于 HSK 等语言标准（详见下表）。

级别	1 级	2 级	3 级
对应级别	HSK1~2 CEFR A1-A2	HSK2~3 CEFR A2-B1	HSK3 CEFR A2-B1
词汇量	300	400	550
字数	2500	3500	4500

为了帮助读者适度地扩大词汇量，每个故事还将出现一定数量的生词，我们对这些生词进行了注音和英文释义，并给出了以应用为主的中文例句。为了方便教师检测汉语教学的效果，我们特别根据IB中文考试的新大纲编写了阅读理解练习题，附在每个故事之后。同时，每册读物均配有24幅生动的插图，这些图片不仅穿插在行文当中，而且还会作为"情节预告"出现在故事的正文之前。图片的巧妙呈现不仅使阅读更加轻松有趣，同时也为教师围绕图片实施教学任务提供了便利条件。读者通过阅读本系列读物，不仅能够迅速地掌握大量常用汉语语料，而且能够稳定地提高阅读理解及口语表达的能力。

　　要想稳步提高阅读水平，课内精读与课外泛读相结合是行之有效的方法之一。"中国智慧故事汉语分级读物"不仅是汉语学习者在课余进行泛读的好朋友，更是汉语教师在课堂上进行阅读教学的好帮手。读故事，学语言，长智慧——"中国智慧故事汉语分级读物"愿与大家在汉语学习的道路上快乐同行！

韩　颖　刘小琳

Preface

China is a country that boasts a diverse culture and enduring civilization. Inspirational stories replete with wisdom can be found throughout her history. Wisdom in Stories: Graded Chinese Readers is a series of carefully selected and entertaining stories that touch on many subjects. These include exceptional moments in the lives of renowned people, detective tactics, military and business strategies, and even innovations in science and technology. The stories are narrated in simple and concise language that is graded by reading difficulty into different levels to meet the learning needs of non-native speakers of the Chinese language. This approach enables readers to enjoy the clever twists and turns of these engaging stories while improving their Chinese.

Wisdom in Stories: Graded Chinese Readers is designed for Chinese learners who are at a middle school or higher level. Each title in this series focuses on one story from contemporary or ancient China, and is graded on a three-level system based on HSK and other established standards. For level 1, the expected Chinese vocabulary of the reader is 300 Chinese words while the total character count for each story is around 2,500. In level 2, the reader is expected to have a grasp of 400 Chinese words while the total character count for each story is around 3,500. For level 3, the numbers are 550 and 4,500 respectively. (See the table below for details.)

Level	1	2	3
Reference Standard	HSK1~2 CEFR A1-A2	HSK2~3 CEFR A2-B1	HSK3 CEFR A2-B1
Vocabulary Words	300	400	550
Character Count	2,500	3,500	4,500

To enable readers to gradually enrich their vocabulary, a limited number of new words are introduced in each story. These are accompanied by pinyin and English translation. In addition, example sentences are also provided to illustrate their usage. After each story, there are also reading exercises designed according to the latest IB Syllabus for Chinese. Instructors and independent learners can use them to assess reading comprehension. Twenty-four vivid and dynamic illustrations also help enhance the plot and serve as a "trailer" for each story. In addition to improving learners' reading experience, the illustrations can be used to design picture-based teaching tasks. Readers will benefit from diverse authentic Chinese texts featuring everyday language that will enable them to steadily increase their skills in reading and speaking.

The combination of intensive reading in class and extensive reading after class is an effective way to develop one's reading skills. Wisdom in Stories: Graded Chinese Readers can serve in both capacities and be of great use to both Chinese language learners and teachers. Stories, language and wisdom — this series hopes to accompany you on an enjoyable journey of learning Chinese.

Han Ying and Liu Xiaolin

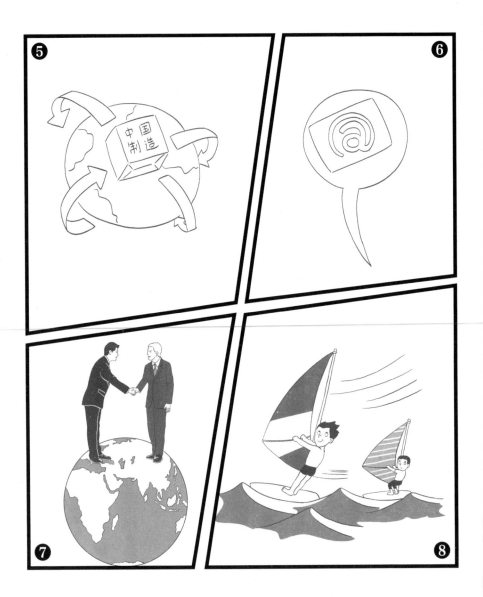

背景和人物简介
Background and Characters

马云（Mǎ Yún）：阿里巴巴集团创始人。
Jack Ma: Founder of Alibaba Group.

蔡崇信（Cài Chóngxìn）：阿里巴巴集团执行副主席。
Joseph Tsai: Executive Vice Chairman of Alibaba.

孙正义（Sūn Zhèngyì）：软件银行集团董事长兼总裁。
Masayoshi Son: Chairman of the Board and President of SoftBank Corporation.

杭州（Hángzhōu）：中国东南沿海的一个城市，马云的家乡。
Hangzhou: A coastal city in southeast China, hometown of Jack Ma.

瑞典（Ruìdiǎn）：一个位于斯堪的纳维亚半岛的国家，北欧五国之一。

Sweden: A country located on the Scandinavian Peninsula, one of the five countries in Northern Europe.

阿里巴巴（Ālǐbābā）：中国的电商巨头，在全球范围内与谷歌、亚马逊、PayPal和eBay等公司齐名。

Alibaba Group: An e-commerce giant in China that enjoys equal fame on the world stage with Google, Amazon, PayPal, eBay, etc.

淘宝（Táobǎo）：中国的一家在线购物网站，是世界上最大的电子商务网站之一。

Taobao: A Chinese online shopping website, which is one of the largest e-commerce websites in the world.

天猫（Tiānmāo）：原名淘宝商城，是一个综合性购物网站。

Tmall: Formerly known as Taobao Mall, a large-scale shopping website that is part of Alibaba.

支付宝（Zhīfùbǎo）：淘宝开发的第三方支付平台，目前有5.2亿用户。

Alipay: A third-party payment platform with 520 million
subscribers as of 2017, developed by Taobao.

高盛（Gāoshèng）：世界领先的投资银行之一。

Goldman Sachs Group: A world-leading investment bank.

马云和阿里巴巴

  马云是中国电商①巨头②阿里巴巴(Alibaba)的创始人③和执行董事长④，可以说是世界⑤上最成功的商人⑥之一。1999年，马云创立⑦了阿里巴巴，现在阿里巴巴旗下⑧有多个电商

① 电商 diànshāng *n.* e-commerce

e.g., 电商就是电子商务的简称。

② 巨头 jùtóu *n.* tycoon; giant

e.g., 你知道"二战"的三巨头都是谁吗？

③ 创始人 chuàngshǐrén *n.* founder

e.g., 扎克伯格是 Facebook 的创始人。

④ 执行董事长 zhíxíng dǒngshìzhǎng *n.*

executive chairman

e.g., 他是公司的执行董事长。

⑤ 世界 shìjiè *n.* world

e.g., 世界上最美丽的女人是谁？

⑥ 商人 shāngrén *n.*

businessman; merchant

e.g., 商人把东西卖给别人。

⑦ 创立 chuànglì *v.* establish; found

e.g., 孔子创立了儒家思想。

⑧ 旗下 qíxià under the banner of

e.g., 这个娱乐公司旗下有很多明星。

网站①，如淘宝、天猫等。

　　1964年，马云在杭州出生。他本来是杭州一所大学②的英文③老师，不上课的时候兼职④当翻译⑤，还开了一家翻译公司⑥。1995年，马云作为翻译第一次去美国⑦，第一次知道了互联网⑧。

①网站 wǎngzhàn *n.* website
e.g., 百度是一个很有名的网站。
②大学 dàxué *n.* university
e.g., 高中毕业之后他考上了北京大学。
③英文 yīngwén *n.* English
e.g., 我在新东方学习英文。
④兼职 jiānzhí *v.* work part-time
e.g., 你想不想兼职当老师？
⑤翻译 fānyì *n.*
translator; interpreter
e.g., 她英文特别好，是我们公司的翻译。
⑥公司 gōngsī *n.* company
e.g., 你在哪家公司工作？
⑦美国 měiguó *n.* United States of America
e.g., 美国是世界上的大国之一。
⑧互联网 hùliánwǎng *n.* Internet
e.g., 互联网把世界上的人连在了一起。

据说，当时马云问美国朋友："什么是互联网？"朋友告诉他："马云，你可以在互联网上搜索①世界上任何②你想要的东西。"马云问："怎么搜索？'搜索'是什么意思？"朋友们说："打字就可以。"

①搜索 sōusuǒ *v.* search
e.g., 中国人经常使用百度进行搜索。
②任何 rènhé *pron.*
any; whatever
e.g., 我爱你超过任何人。

他们让马云试一试^①。马云开始还不敢^②碰^③电脑^④，因为在那个时候，电脑非常贵，马云怕^⑤万一碰坏了电脑，他可赔^⑥不起。朋友们对他说："没事儿，你就用吧！"马云才小心翼翼^⑦地开始搜索。

马云第一个搜索的是英文单词"啤酒^⑧"。他找到了美国、德国、日本等各个国家的啤酒，但是没有中国的啤酒。他第二个搜索的是英

① 试 shì v. try

e.g., 你试试这双鞋。

② 敢 gǎn v. dare

e.g., 那条路太黑了，她不敢走。

③ 碰 pèng v. touch

e.g., 那个有电，你不要碰。

④ 电脑 diànnǎo n. computer

e.g., 他妈妈给他买了一台新电脑。

⑤ 怕 pà v. fear; be afraid

e.g., 你让别人帮你写吧，我怕我写不好。

⑥ 赔 péi v. compensate

e.g., 你弄坏了东西就得赔。

⑦ 小心翼翼 xiǎoxīnyìyì

with much caution

e.g., 她小心翼翼地走了出去。

⑧ 啤酒 píjiǔ n. beer

e.g., 老王很喜欢喝啤酒。

文单词"中国"，结果还是什么都没搜出来。

要知道，中国可是占世界上人口四分之一的大国啊，互联网上竟然①没有中国的东西！这让马云很吃惊，也很难受。就在那个时候，不懂互联网的马云决定在中国开一个互联网公司，做电商生意②，把中国的商品卖到全世界！

①竟然 jìngrán adv.
unexpectedly
e.g., 你竟然不知道这件事！
②生意 shēngyi n. business
e.g., 阿里巴巴让天下没有难做的生意。

说干就干，马云回国后就请人给自己的翻译公司做了一个很小很简单的网站。网站上线①当天，马云接②到朋友的电话③。朋友叫道："老马，你收到了五封电子邮件④！"马云问："电子邮件是什么？"

①上线 shàngxiàn v.
be launched
e.g., 我们公司的官网下个月上线。
②接 jiē v. receive; answer (a phone call)
e.g., 你帮我接一下快递。
③电话 diànhuà n.
phone call
e.g., 有人打电话找你。
④电子邮件 diànzǐ yóujiàn n.
email
e.g., 有事的话给我发电子邮件。

后来马云赶到公司，看到邮件中写到:"你们在哪里，我们可以合作① 吗？"马云非常高兴，他相信互联网可以改变世界！后来马云从大学辞了职②，一心一意地做互联网。

①合作 hézuò v. cooperate

e.g., 你们俩合作得挺好。

②辞职 cízhí v.

quit one`s job

e.g., 老板，我要辞职！

1999 年，35 岁的马云凑^①了 50 万，创立了阿里巴巴网站。

在工作中，马云认识了一家瑞典投资^②公司的高管^③：蔡崇信。马云跟蔡崇信讲^④了自己的梦想，讲了阿里巴巴。蔡崇信觉得阿里巴巴是一个很难得的模式^⑤，马云觉得蔡崇信是一个做事的人。

①凑 còu v. collect; scratch together

e.g., 咱们能凑个首付。

②投资 tóuzī n. investment

e.g., 你能给我多少投资？

③高管 gāoguǎn n. high executive

e.g., 他是联想的高管。

④讲 jiǎng v. tell

e.g., 给我讲一讲你的故事吧。

⑤模式 móshì n. mode; model

e.g., 这个模式不适合我们。

蔡崇信跟马云谈了四天，最后他对马云说：“马云，那边我不干了，我要加入①阿里巴巴！”马云说：“你来，就帮我管②钱吧，但是我每个月只能给你500元的工资③。”蔡崇信说："没问题。"就这样，蔡崇信放弃④了年薪⑤70万美元⑥的工作，成为了阿里巴巴的首席财务官⑦。

①加入 jiārù v. join; take part
e.g., 我们要创业，你要加入我们吗？

②管 guǎn v. manage; handle
e.g., 你能不能好好管管你家孩子？

③工资 gōngzī n. salary; wage
e.g., 你的工资是多少？

④放弃 fàngqì v. give up
e.g., 你不要放弃，还有我们！

⑤年薪 niánxīn n. annual salary
e.g., 老王家的孩子年薪50万，真了不起！

⑥美元 měiyuán n. US dollar
e.g., 美国的货币是美元。

⑦首席财务官 shǒuxí cáiwùguān
n. chief financial officer
e.g., 首席财务官负责公司的财务和会计事务。

因为互联网是一个烧^①钱的行业^②，马云开始四处寻找投资人。然而，他被风险^③投资拒绝^④了37次。后来马云幽默^⑤地说，是他拒绝了投资人的投资。阿里巴巴的老员工^⑥说，当时连最基本的500块的工资都发^⑦不出了。马云还是坚持着。

① 烧 shāo *v.* burn; cost
e.g., 你在房地产上烧钱是不是疯了？

② 行业 hángyè *n.* industry; profession
e.g., 她不知道自己将来该从事什么行业。

③ 风险 fēngxiǎn *n.* risk
e.g., 把所有的钱都放到股市里风险太大了。

④ 拒绝 jùjué *v.* refuse; rebuff
e.g., 她拒绝跟我一起出去吃饭。

⑤ 幽默 yōumò *adj.* humorous
e.g., 他是一个很幽默的人，经常讲笑话。

⑥ 员工 yuángōng *n.* staff; employee
e.g., 这个公司有52个员工。

⑦ 发 fā *v.* send out
e.g., 来参加活动的人，每人发一个纪念品。

1999 年 10 月，高盛联合 ① 其他几家公司给阿里巴巴投了 500 万美元，马云松了一口气。10 月 31 日，马云得到了一个和世界级风险投资家孙正义见面的机会。那天，马云没穿西装 ②，没想从孙正义那里拿到钱，因为他刚拿到了高盛投的 500 万美元。

①联合 liánhé v.
unite; ally with
e.g., 让我们联合起来，共同奋斗！
②西装 xīzhuāng n.
suit (Western-style)
e.g., 他穿着一套白色的西装。

马云向孙正义讲了自己的梦想。他说阿里巴巴做的是电子商务，就是要把中国的商品卖到全世界，还讲了他对互联网的看法。没有想到，短短的六分钟之后，孙正义就决定要给阿里巴巴投资。孙正义认为，中国将会成为全球 GDP 最大的国家，阿里巴巴面对的是全球市场，而不仅仅是中国市场。马云创立的阿里巴巴将会是第一家真正的中国互联网公司。

孙正义对马云说:"你要多少钱?"

马云说:"我不要钱。"

孙正义说:"怎么能不要钱呢!"

马云说:"我真的不要钱……"

孙正义说:"这样吧,我给你投4000万美元。"

马云说:"不不不,我最多才管过200万元人民币,4000万美元我不要。"

孙正义说:"你一定得要这4000万。"

马云说："我回去考虑①一下。"

马云后来问孙正义："为什么当年你只用了六分钟时间，就决定投资 4000 万美元给阿里巴巴？"

孙正义回答："我见到你的时候，你什么都没有，中国的互联网也是刚起步。但是，你是一个有梦想和激情的聪明人，所以，我决定投资你的公司。"

①考虑 kǎolǜ v. consider; think over
e.g., 这个问题我要好好考虑一下。

马云后来幽默地说："从那一天起，他喜欢上了我，我也喜欢上了他。后来他身边的人说我们俩是灵魂伴侣①。有人不相信一见钟情②，也许那就是一见钟情，这是真实的事情。"

但是马云回杭州后，又后悔①了，"我要那么多钱干什么呢？真是太愚蠢②了。我不会用，这样下去公司要出问题的。"

这个时候，孙正义派人去跟马云说，一定要见马云。于是马云就带着蔡崇信坐飞机③到日本，跟孙正义继续谈投资的事。

①后悔 hòuhuǐ v. regret
e.g., 我从不后悔。
②愚蠢 yúchǔn adj. silly
e.g., 你这么做是愚蠢的行为！
③飞机 fēijī n. plane; flight
e.g., 我明天坐飞机去上海。

孙正义说:"马云,我还是要给你 4000 万美元。"

马云坐在那里不说话。蔡崇信说:"不行。"

孙正义吓了一跳。因为大多数人都是怕投资人给的钱少,没有说投资人给的钱太多的。就这样,孙正义出了三次价,蔡崇信都拒绝了。

最后大家口头说好，孙正义给阿里巴巴投资 2000 万美元。

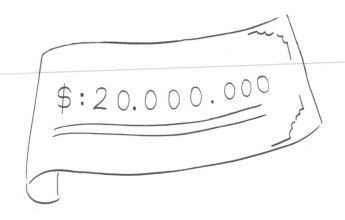

马云后来说，不接受那么多钱，是因为阿里当时的规模①根本用不了那么多钱，一个公司如果有太多的钱，那是一件很危险②的事情！

聪明③人不会只看眼前利益④。

① 规模 guīmó *n.*

scope; size

e.g., 这个工厂规模不大。

② 危险 wēixiǎn *adj.*

dangerous; risky

e.g., 你不要过去，太危险了。

③ 聪明 cōngmíng *adj.* clever;

smart

e.g., 她的女儿很聪明。

④ 利益 lìyì *n.* interest; benefit

e.g., 大家要保护自己的利益。

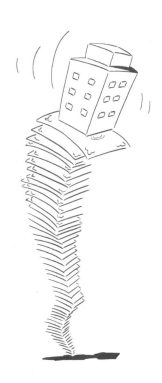

马云后来说到他和<u>孙正义</u>的那次见面，幽默地说："我是那种看起来很聪明、实际①上不聪明的人。那哥们儿看起来不聪明，但他是很聪明的人，真正是有大智慧②的人。"

① 实际 shíjì *n.* reality; actual condition
e.g.，实际上他没有告诉我任何有价值的信息。
② 智慧 zhìhuì *n.* wisdom
e.g.，他是一个很有智慧的人。

2001 年底，<u>孙正义</u>到北京来开会，他投资的三十几家互联网公司的负责人都要参加。<u>孙正义</u>给他们每人 15 分钟，讲自己公司的发展情况。当时三十几家公司基本上都换了方向，都不说自己是互联网公司了，而且讲了很长时间。

马云最后一个讲，他只说了几句话："孙先生，我向你要钱时是这个梦想，今天我告诉你，我还是这个梦想。唯一的区别是，我向我的梦想走近了一步，我还在往前走。"

马云离他的梦想越来越近。淘宝网 2003 年推出的第三方支付[1]平台[2]——支付宝是"中国新四大发明[1]"之一。2016 年，阿里巴巴成为世界上最大的零售[3]商。2018 年，阿里巴巴的市值[4]约为 5000 亿美元。

①支付 zhīfù v. pay

e.g., 手机支付现在很流行。

②平台 píngtái n. platform

e.g., 我们能给你一个很大的发展平台。

③零售 língshòu v. retail

e.g., 这家店不零售，只批发。

④市值 shìzhí n.

market value

e.g., 市值就是股票总价值。

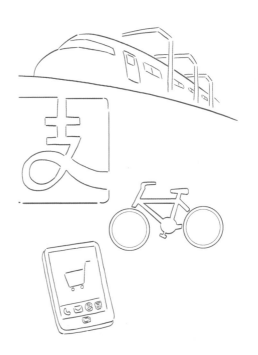

马云说过:"一个聪明的人看到的是别人看不到的东西,一个有智慧的人看到的是自己假装没看到的东西。聪明的人知道自己要什么,有智慧的人知道自己不要什么。"

马云能发现机会,把握机会,坚持努力,是一个有智慧的人。

1.中国新四大发明

2017年5月,来自"一带一路"沿线的20国青年评选出了中国的"新四大发明",分别是高铁、支付宝、共享单车和网购。

Jack Ma and His Alibaba Dream

Jack Ma(Ma Yun), founder and Executive Chairman of China's e-commerce giant Alibaba Group, can be considered one of the world's most successful businessmen. In 1999, he established Alibaba Group, which now includes several e-commerce websites like Taobao and Tmall.

Jack Ma was born in Hangzhou in 1964. He originally worked as an English teacher at a university in his hometown and worked part-time as an interpreter, eventually opening a company providing translation services. In 1995, he made his first trip to the United States as an interpreter, where he came to know the Internet for the first time.

The story goes, he asked his American friends, "What is the Internet?" They told him, "Jack, it is where you can search for anything you want in the world." Ma went on asking, "How do you search? And what does 'search' mean?" He was told, "Just type."

His friends wanted him to try using a computer, but he didn't dare to touch one. Back then, computers were very expensive and he was afraid that if he were to cause any damage to one, he wouldn't be able to pay to fix it. But his friends told him,

"It's no problem, just try it." Proceeding very cautiously, he began searching for information.

The first English word Jack Ma searched was "beer", from which he found information about beer made in various countries such as the US, Germany and Japan. But he didn't see anything about Chinese beer. The second word he tried was "China". Unfortunately, there were no results.

One has to bear in mind that China is a large country that takes up one-fourth of the world's population. Yet nothing about the country could be found on the Internet! Ma was shocked by this fact and felt very sad. From that moment, Jack Ma, who knew little about the Internet, made up his mind to establish an Internet company in China that would be engaged in e-commerce so that Chinese goods could be sold all over the world.

Actions speak louder than words. Upon returning to China, Ma commissioned someone to design a rather simple website for his translation company. On the day it was launched, Ma received a phone call from his friend. His friend told him in excitement, "Ma, you've got five emails!" "What are emails?" Ma replied.

He then rushed to his company to read the emails, one of

which said, "Where is your company? Can we cooperate?" Overjoyed, he began to believe that the Internet could bring about changes to the world! Subsequently, he quit his job at the university and devoted himself to his Internet business.

In 1999, the 35-year-old Jack Ma raised 500,000RMB yuan and founded Alibaba.com.

Through his work, Ma came to know Joseph Tsai, an executive at a Swedish investment company. He told Tsai about his dream and the company he had established, Alibaba. Tsai thought Alibaba's business model was quite unique. To Ma, Tsai was indeed a man of action.

The two discussed business for four straight days. By the end of it, Tsai said to Ma, "Jack, I want to quit my current job and join Alibaba." Ma replied, "If you can, just help me manage the company's wealth. But I'm sorry that I can only guarantee you a monthly salary of 500 yuan." Tsai replied, "No problem." Thus Joseph Tsai gave up a position that saw him earn an annual salary of 700,000 US dollars to become the Chief Financial Officer of Alibaba.

Because you can burn a lot of money working in the Internet industry, Ma then began a search for investors. To his dismay, he was refused 37 times by venture capital investment companies. He said jokingly later that it was he who rebuffed their investment. According to some senior employees of Alibaba, back then, the company was unable to pay them even the basic monthly wage of 500 yuan. But he was still working on it.

In October 1999, the Goldman Sachs Group, along with several other companies, invested five million US dollars in Alibaba. This helped ease a lot of pressure on Jack Ma. On October 31, he got a chance to meet with Masayoshi Son, a world-renowned venture capital investor. He didn't wear a Western-style suit that day, because he had just received the five million US dollars of investment from Goldman Sachs and thus didn't expect anything from Son.

Ma told Son about his dream. He said that Alibaba, as an e-commerce company, aimed to sell Chinese products worldwide. He also briefed Son about his views on the Internet. To his surprise, Son decided to invest in Alibaba after having listened to him for just six minutes. Son believed that China as a country would one day have the world's highest GDP. Alibaba had set its eyes on not only the Chinese market, but also the whole globe. Son thought Alibaba, the company founded by Jack Ma, would be China's first Internet corporation in the real sense.

Son asked Ma, "How much money do you want?"

Ma replied, "I don't want money."

Son was surprised and said, "How come you don't need money?"

Ma said, "No, I don't want any money…."

Son said, "How about I invest 40 million US dollars?"

Ma replied, "No, no. Two million yuan is the highest I've ever managed. I can't handle 40 million dollars."

However, Son insisted, "Please accept my 40 million dollars."

Ma said, "I need to go back and think it over."

Many years after having accepted the investment, Ma asked Son, "Why did you make the decision to invest 40 million dollars in Alibaba after only a six-minute conversation between us?"

Son answered, "When we first met, you were no more than a self-made businessman and China's Internet industry was in its early stage. But I quickly realized you were a smart person with a dream and passion. That's why I made up my mind to invest in your company."

Later on, Ma said in a joking way, "From that day on, we fell in love with each other. His intimate colleagues once said we are like soul mates. Some people don't believe in love at first sight, but that was what happened between us. "

However, after accepting the money from Son, Ma regretted his decision upon returning to Hangzhou. He thought, "Why did I accept so much money as an investment? That was so silly of me! I have no idea how to use all that money, so the company will run into trouble sooner or later."

At that juncture, Son sent his aide to tell Ma that he wanted to meet him again in person. Ma thus took a flight to Japan along with Joseph Tsai to continue to discuss with Son about the investment.

Son insisted, "Jack, I still want to give you 40 million dollars."

Ma sat in his seat, silent. Tsai then spoke up, "We won't accept it."

Son was astonished because he thought most people would want as much investment as they could get. He made three offers, but they were all refused by Tsai.

Finally, the three reached an oral agreement that Son would invest 30 million dollars in Alibaba.

Ma explained later on that given the company's limited size at the time, they didn't need such a large investment. To a company, too much money would mean too much risk!

A smart person would not focus on the short-term benefit.

Speaking of his encounter with Son, Ma once said with humor, "I'm that kind of person who appears to be smart, but who is slow-witted in essence; Son seems to have nothing special, but he is in fact a very bright person, a man with great wisdom."

At the end of 2001, Masayoshi Son went to Beijing to attend a conference. The people who were in charge of over 30 Internet companies he had invested in were all invited. Son allowed each of them 15 minutes to talk about the situation at their companies. Few of the executives still called their businesses Internet companies, as most of them had changed business models. They all spoke for quite a while.

Jack Ma was the last one to speak. He only made a few remarks, "Mr. Son, I had a dream when I discussed investment with you. Today, I can tell you my dream remains the same. The only difference is that I'm now one step closer to realizing that dream, and I'm still marching forward."

Indeed, Jack Ma is coming closer and closer to realizing his dream. Alipay, a third-party payment platform launched by Taobao in 2003, is regarded as one of "China's four great inventions in the new era". In 2016, Alibaba became the world's largest e-commerce retailer. In 2018, its market value is estimated at 500 billion US dollars.

Ma once said, "A smart person sees what others cannot see, and a wise man sees what he pretends not to see. A smart person knows what he wants, while a wise man is aware of what he doesn't need."

With the ability to find an opportunity, seize it and persistently pursue it, Jack Ma himself is such a person who possesses great wisdom.

China's four great inventions in the new era:

In May 2017, youth from 20 countries along the route of the "Belt and Road" Initiative selected "China's four great inventions in the new era", namely the high-speed railway, Alipay, shared bicycles and online shopping.

一 根据故事内容给下列各题选择一个正确的答案。
Choose the correct answer according to the story.

1. 马云出生在哪里? (　　)

　A. 北京　　　B. 杭州　　　C. 日本　　　D. 美国

2. 马云在哪一年创立了阿里巴巴? (　　)

　A. 1995 年　B. 1999 年　C. 2000 年　D. 2003 年

3. 蔡崇信为什么加入阿里巴巴? (　　)

　　A. 阿里巴巴的工资高

　　B. 阿里巴巴的假期多

　　C. 阿里巴巴的发展模式好

　　D. 阿里巴巴让他当首席财务官

4. 孙正义最后给了马云多少风险投资? (　　)

　　A. 200 万人民币　　　　B. 2000 万美元

　　C. 3000 万美元　　　　D. 4000 万美元

5. 下面哪一个不是"中国新四大发明"? (　　)

　　A. 网购　　　　　　　B. 共享单车

　　C. 微博　　　　　　　D. 支付宝

二 从故事的第三段中，找出与下列词语意思最接近的一个词语。

Find the synonyms for the following words in the third paragraph of the story.

例：美丽　　漂亮

1. 全球　　＿＿＿＿＿＿＿
2. 寻找　　＿＿＿＿＿＿＿

三 根据故事，从下列选项中选出三个正确的叙述。

Choose three correct statements based on your understanding of the story.

A. 马云本来是一个大学的英文老师。

B. 马云刚学会上网的时候，发现网上没有中国的商品。

C. 马云在 1999 年创立了阿里巴巴。

D. 马云向孙正义要 4000 万美元，但是孙正义只给了马云 2000 万美元。

E. 马云认为自己是一个有智慧的人。

选词填空。
Choose the appropriate words to fill in the blanks.

马云第一个搜索的是英文单词"啤酒"，_____ 他找到了美国、德国、日本等各个国家的啤酒，_____ 没有中国的啤酒。他第二个搜索的是英文单词"中国"，结果 _____ 什么都没搜出来。

要知道，中国可是占世界上人口四分之一的大国啊，在互联网上 _____ 没有中国的东西！这让马云很吃惊，也很难受。就在那个时候，不懂互联网的马云决定在中国开一个互联网公司，做电商生意，把中国的商品卖到全世界！

A. 竟然　　　B. 但是　　　C. 还是　　　D. 然后

看图说话：请用中文描述下面这张图片的内容，尽量说清人物、背景和事件经过，可以加上你自己对人物或事件的看法及评价。

Describe the following picture in Chinese, including the characters, background information and plot. You can also add your comments on the characters or the story.

简答题。

Answer the following question succinctly .

你觉得马云是一个有智慧的人吗？为什么？

课后练习答案Keys to the exercises

一、根据故事内容给下列各题选择一个正确的答案。
　　1. B　2. B　3. C　4. B　5. C

二、从故事的第三段中，找出与下列词语意思最接近的
　　一个词语。
　　1. 世界　　2. 搜索

三、根据故事，从下列选项中选出三个正确的叙述。
　　A　B　C

四、选词填空。
　　D　B　C　A

五、看图说话。
　　略

六、简答题。
　　略

项目策划：刘小琳　韩　颖
责任编辑：李婷晓
英文编辑：范逊敏
插图绘制：硕果儿
封面设计：何思倩　牛慧珍

图书在版编目（CIP）数据

马云和阿里巴巴：汉英对照 / 刘小琳编著；薛彧威译. --
北京：华语教学出版社，2018.8
（中国智慧故事汉语分级读物）
ISBN 978-7-5138-1613-7

Ⅰ．①马… Ⅱ．①刘… ②薛… Ⅲ．①汉语－对外汉语教
学－语言读物 Ⅳ．① H195.5

中国版本图书馆 CIP 数据核字 (2018) 第 169987 号

马云和阿里巴巴

刘小琳　编著　薛彧威　翻译

*

©华语教学出版社有限责任公司
华语教学出版社有限责任公司出版
（中国北京百万庄大街24号　邮政编码 100037）
电话：(86)10-68320585　68997826
传真：(86)10-68997826　68326333
网址：www.sinolingua.com.cn
电子信箱：hyjx@sinolingua.com.cn
北京玺诚印务有限公司印刷
2018年（32开）第1版
2018年第1版第1次印刷
（汉英）
ISBN 978-7-5138-1613-7
定价：16.90元